The Water
D0370947
Story & Art by
Rei Toma
10

The Water Dragon God

The god who rules over the waters. Though he hates humans, he is intrigued by Asahi and feels compassion for her.

Asahi

She was transported to another world when she was young. Subaru's mother sacrificed her to the water dragon god.

Subaru

He is drawn to Asahi and has resolved to protect her.

Kogahiko

He's seeking the water dragon god's power by targeting Asahi.

The Emperor

A young boy, the emperor of the country of Naga.

Tsukihiko

Asahi's caretaker. He has the ability to sense people's thoughts and emotions.

Hino

The daughter of the family who took Kurose in. She died during the war.

Kurose

His heart was plunged into darkness, and there he discovered Tokoyami.

Tokoyami

The god of darkness. He summons Kurose from the modern-day world.

STORY THUS FAR

◎ Asahi is living a normal, sheltered life when she suddenly gets pulled into a pond and is transported to a strange new world. She gets sacrificed to a water dragon god, and he takes her voice from her. Because of her connection to the water dragon god's mysterious powers, Asahi is elevated to the position of priestess in her village. She is unable to find a way to return home, and time passes. As Asahi and the water dragon god spend time together, their relationship begins to change.

◎ A priestess of Naga informs the emperor of Asahi's and the water dragon god's existence, so he orders Asahi to lend him her power. When Kogahiko tries to kidnap Asahi a second time, the water dragon god and Asahi's friends rescue her. Tsukihiko, whose mother was in the same situation as Asahi before, attempts to trade his life for Asahi's freedom.

◎ The emperor of Naga asks for Asahi's hand in marriage. In order to protect Asahi, the water dragon god sends her back to her own world. Asahi is finally reunited with her family, but she can't forget the water dragon god and the friends she's left behind. She's so troubled that she returns to the other world during a ceremony to call rain.

◎ Meanwhile, a young man named Kurose in the modern-day world is plunged into darkness. The god of darkness, Tokoyami, places Kurose in this other world where Kurose gets a measure of peace. Unfortunately, war with a neighboring country causes Kurose to lose Hino, the person he cares most about, so he joins Tokoyami in his schemes. They place Kogahiko as the new emperor, and Kogahiko kidnaps Asahi once again. Subaru brings an army to rescue Asahi, and Asahi feels powerless as she watches the battle unfold. Suddenly, the water dragon god gives his power to her!

The Water Dragon's Bride

10

CONTENTS

CHAPTER
37

It's volume 10!
Ryohei Kimura graciously voiced the water dragon god in a special promo video for The Water Dragon's Bride a little while ago, and he was kind enough to do it again for the special drama CD packaged with the Japanese magazine! There weren't very many lines for the water dragon god in the promo, and I regretted not giving him more to say. This time, I got to listen to the water dragon god's voice much more, and I'm so happy! It's a somewhat unique plot, with the water dragon god listening to maidens' worries. Ha ha. When I read about the scenario, I was a little worried about how to have him give them advice without destroying his character, and it was a bit hard... I worried over it more than I worry over the manga's plot! Ha ha.
Earth God

WOW ...
SHE'S... DIVINE...

ASAHI.
WHO COULD SAY THAT YOU HAVE NO POWER?
THE ONLY ONE...
...WHO COULD SPUR THIS GOD TO MOVE...
...IS YOU.

USE...
...ME.

PWSH
AHH ...!
AH...
FWSH

LADY
PRIEST-
ESS...!

Nhn...
TMP
...

KOGA-HIKO.
LOOK AT THIS.
WHAT MADE YOU WANT TO GET MORE POWER-FUL?
IF YOU THROW AWAY THE PEOPLE WHO'VE FOUGHT FOR YOU, WHERE WILL THEY GO?

HUG
FWSH
FWUUU

AH...
PLEASE, LADY PRIESTESS, HELP KOGAHIKO!
KOGAHIKO IS WORKING SO HARD FOR US...
...SO WE HAVE TO WORK HARD TOO...
VSH
NGH...
VSHH
KOGA-HIKO?!

KOGA-HIKO!
AHHH...
I'M AWAKE NOW...

WE CAN'T CONTROL THAT ONE ANY LONGER.
TCH.
WE MUST SPREAD THE DARKNESS... MORE BROADLY ...
YOU WANT THAT PRIESTESS AND THE WATER DRAGON GOD TO SUFFER, DON'T YOU?
...?
WE STILL HAVE PAWNS...

WE'LL USE THAT EMPEROR INSTEAD...
VSH
I WON'T LET YOU!
GH...
GLUB

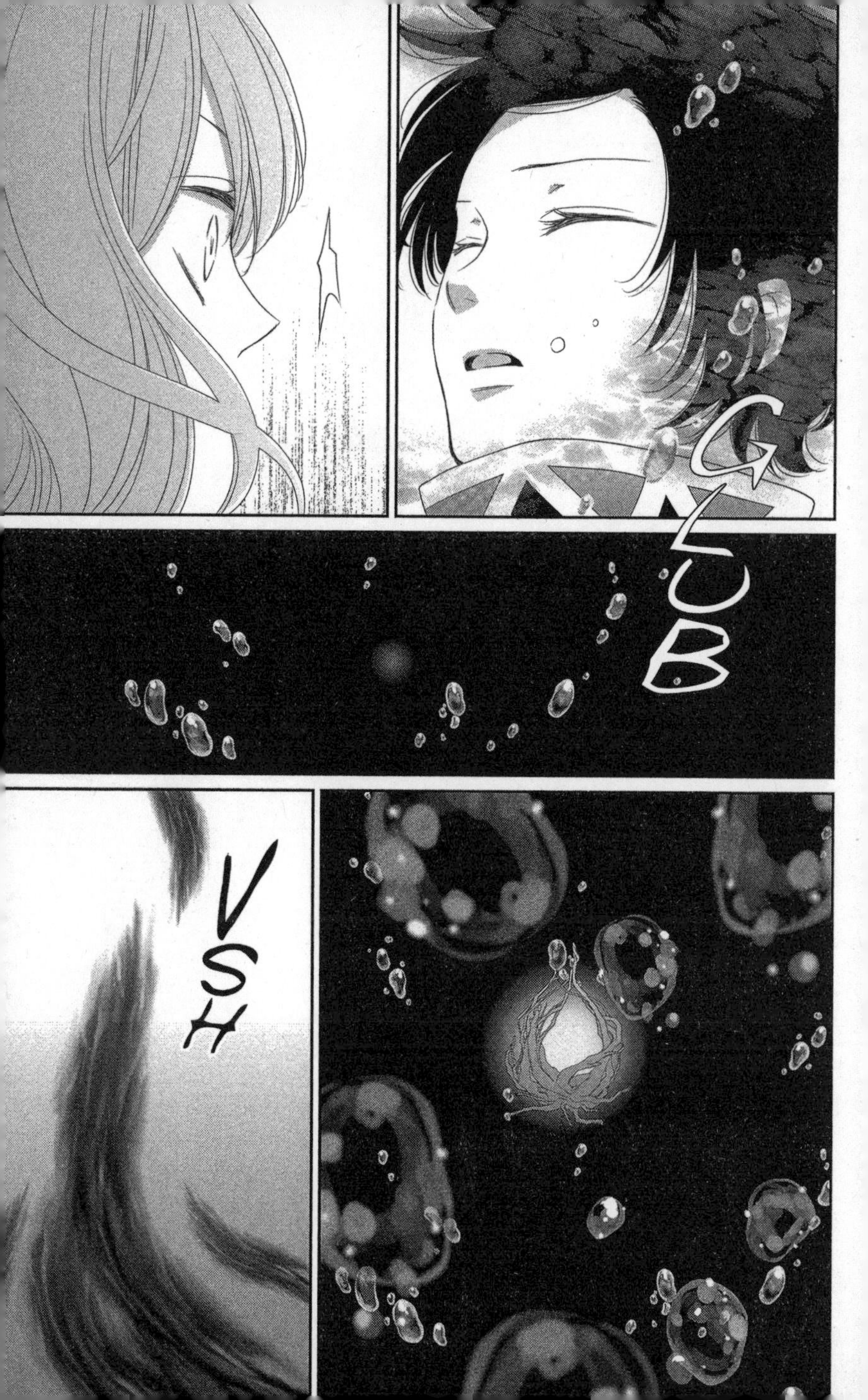
GLUB
VSH

VSH
SHP
ASAHI ...!
FWSH
WATER DRAGON GOD?

YOU'RE
...
...GOING TO HELP, AREN'T YOU?
You want me to get in this thing?
Master
...
Please go, quickly...
WATER DRAGON GOD.
THANK YOU...
...FOR COMING.

THAT'S AN EMPEROR FOR YOU.
EVEN AS SMALL AND POWERLESS AS YOU ARE, YOU STILL STRUGGLE AGAINST MY DARKNESS.
WHO ARE YOU ...?
YOU SHOULD BE HONORED. THE GOD OF DARKNESS IS LENDING YOU A BIT OF HIS POWER.
GOD OF DARK-NESS?
I SEE... SO THIS UNSETTLING SENSATION LIKE I'M GOING TO ROT AWAY IS YOUR DOING THEN...
AND YOU'RE REPON-SIBLE FOR MY BROTHER —!

I LENT POWER TO THE JEALOUSY HE ALREADY HARBORED.
IT WAS MERELY A PUSH IN THE RIGHT DIRECTION.
SHF
IF YOU FIND HIM SO UNWORTHY...
...THEN ALLOW ME TO HAVE THE EMPEROR'S THRONE.
BROTHER...
I WILL SHOW YOU THAT I CAN BE A SUPERIOR EMPEROR TO MY YOUNGER BROTHER.
GOD OF DARKNESS, I BESEECH YOU...
HRM...

IN THAT CASE, WE NO LONGER HAVE NEED OF THIS PAWN.
LEAVING HIM ALIVE WOULD ONLY CAUSE MORE PROBLEMS, SO WE SHOULD KILL HIM.
HE SHOULD JUST ROT AWAY.
LET'S MAKE SURE HE NEVER LEAVES THIS UNDER-WORLD.
VSH

HEY... THIS CAN BE YOUR FIRST JOB AS EMPEROR.
LET'S CRUSH THIS SEED OF REBELLION BEFORE IT CAN SPROUT.
SHA
YES.
BRO... THER...
GRP

DIE!!
I WISH YOU HAD NEVER BEEN BORN...!
GH...
HAVE YOU...
...ALWAYS...
...DESPISED ME SO MUCH...?
YES...! MY WEAK LITTLE BROTHER REIGNING OVER ME...
IT'S MADE ME MISERABLE MY ENTIRE LIFE!

THEN WHY HAVE YOU STAYED BY MY SIDE?
WHY ARE YOU ONLY TRYING TO KILL ME NOW?
YOU COULD HAVE... KILLED ME ANY-TIME...
YOU WOULDN'T HAVE STAYED WITH ME...
...IF YOU HATED ME THIS MUCH.
GHK...
PLEASE... OPEN YOUR EYES... BROTHER...

YOU TURNED AWAY FROM YOUR OWN DESIRES, YOUR HATRED...
...AND YOU STAYED WITH ME.
YOU'RE A STRONG AND KIND MAN, BROTHER.

AH... AH...
WHEEZ
THAT'S... RIGHT... I THOUGHT ...
...MY HATRED WAS THE SMALLEST OF THORNS IN MY HEART, AND YET...
THMP
BIG BROTHER ...
I KNEW HE WOULD BE FOUND LACKING.
WE MUST FIND ONE WHO'S EASIER TO MISLEAD... ONE WHO HOLDS A DEEP DARKNESS IN THEIR HEART.
TCH.
WHAT IS...?
PLSH
WATER?

SPL
SHY
?!
AGAIN... HOW CAN YOU ENTER HERE...?!

THE LAST TIME I CAME, I LEFT SOME WATER BEHIND.
HEH... HEH HEH HEH.
HA HA HA!

I LIKE THAT LOOK ON YOUR FACE...
...WATER DRAGON GOD.
THAT CONFUSION ITSELF IS MY SUSTENANCE.
MY JOY.
HEH HEH ...
THIS IS FUN.
YOUR MAJESTY! ARE YOU ALL RIGHT?
WE'RE FINE.

...
DASH
?!
WHERE ARE YOU GOING? TRYING TO RUN?!
VM
TOKO-YAMI?!
...

STOP!!

AH.
YOU SAW IT AS WELL, THEN.
YES.
I SAW IT BACK THEN...
THE REASON THAT GUY... KUROSE... WAS SWALLOWED BY THE DARKNESS ...
WAIT...!
TOKO-YAMI!
THERE ...

WHAT THE—

HINO...

I'M OLD ENOUGH TO GET MARRIED IF I WANT ...!
I WANTED SACRIFICES...
...SO I WANTED CHAOS.

YES.
THAT'S RIGHT...
WHY DID I...
...FORGET SOMETHING...
...SO IMPORTANT...?
WHY...
WHY...?

TOKO-
YAMIIIIII
!!
YOU...

YOU HAVE TO BRING HINO BACK TO LIFE!
YOU PROMISED, DIDN'T YOU?!
I'VE CREATED ENOUGH DISORDER... I'VE GROWN DARKNESS FOR YOU.
WE'VE HARVESTED MORE THAN ENOUGH SACRIFICES !!
TO BRING ONE WHO HAS DIED...
...BACK TO LIFE...
...IS SOMETHING THAT NOT EVEN THE GOD OF THE UNDER-WORLD CAN DO.

YOU WERE ONLY BEING USED.
THIS GIRL IS ALREADY ...

HI...NO...
PLUP
FSSH

HINO...
HI...NO...
HINO...
SLUMP

HA...
HEH... HEH HEH HEH...
SH A
WHAT WONDERFUL DARK-NESS!

CHAPTER
38

I FORGOT SOMETHING ...
...IMPORTANT.
THAT'S WHY...
NO, WAIT.
EVEN THOUGH I FORGOT...
IF IT WAS ALL...
...TO BRING YOU BACK...
...THEN I COULD BEAR ALL OF THE...
...HORRIBLE SINS I'VE COMMITTED.

BUT...
...THERE WAS NO POINT.
I FORGOT YOU.
ALL I HAVE LEFT IS MY REGRETS...
...SHINING WHITE IN THE DARKNESS.
BRINGING...
...PAIN INSIDE ME.
NGH...

VSH VSH
...
A MAGNIFICENT DARKNESS...
HUMANS ARE SO SPLENDID ...
THEY'RE THE ONLY CREATURES WHO COULD EVER...
...BRING FORTH A DARKNESS LIKE THIS.

YES...
THAT'S IT...
HEH HEH HEH ...
SHA
BECOME MY NOURISH-MENT.
AND I WILL COVER...
...THIS ENTIRE WORLD IN DARKNESS.
VWSH
VWSH

VWSHH
AH...!
VSHH

BWSH
VSHHH
WHAT ...?
MURMUR
THE SKY IS GROWING DARK...

THIS SEEMS KIND OF OMINOUS ...
UNH...!!
GRAAAH!!
AGH!!
WHAT IS THIS...?
MURMUR
KOGAHIKO, I'M SCARED.
MURMUR

AH!
EVERY-ONE, CALM DOWN!
DON'T LET YOURSELF BE SWALLOWED BY THE DARK-NESS.
JUST HOLD ON, ALL RIGHT?
YEAH
...
I'M COUNT-ING ON YOU...
...ASAHI.

AHH...
I AM FILLED WITH DARKNESS.
MAY IT SWALLOW YOU ALL...
GOD OF DARKNESS, ISN'T IT ABOUT TIME...
...YOU ENDED ALL THIS?
SILENCE...
...WATER GOD.
BOWSH

I'VE TIRED OF THIS...
...UNDER-WORLD.
YOU COULD NEVER UNDER-STAND...
...THIS ...
...

VSH
VSH
FOOL-ISH...
...AND WEAK CHILD OF MAN...
VSH

YOU TOO WILL BE ABSORBED INTO MY DARK-NESS...
...AND BECOME ONE WITH ME.
VWSHH
VWSH
YOU PLAN TO MAKE HIM A SACRI-FICE?

OH NO, YOU DON'T!
ASAHI!!
BW
SH

VSHH
NGH
...
SHIVER
GRIP

GET AWAY FROM THERE, ASAHI!
YOU'RE BEING COVERED WITH HIS MIASMA.
KUROSE!
GET AHOLD OF YOUR-SELF!
KUROSE ...!!

"KUROSE!"
HINO...
HINO...
I'M SORRY...
I'M SORRY THAT I...

TWITCH
HI... NO?
KUROSE!
WATER... PRIEST-ESS...
DON'T LET YOURSELF BE SWALLOWED BY THE DARKNESS!

I...
...DON'T CARE ANY-MORE.
KUROSE!
HEH HEH HEH...
THE GIRL, TOO, WILL BECOME A PART OF ME.
LET ME GO.
NO!
IF I LET YOU GO, I'LL REGRET IT TOO MUCH!
VSH
VSH
VSH

HA HA...
REGRET... THAT'S ALL I'VE GOT.
MY REGRETS... SHINING WHITE IN THE DARK-NESS.
EVERY-THING BUT THAT HAS BEEN PAINTED OVER BY DARK-NESS...
IT'S SUCH A PAIN.
IT'S BECAUSE YOU HAD HOPE!
YOU REFUSED TO LET GO OF YOUR HOPE FROM THAT TIME!

WHITE...
...SHINING...
...AND PAINFUL.
IF I HAD ACKNOWLEDGED MY POWER AS A PRIESTESS EARLIER...
IF I HADN'T TURNED AWAY FROM THE FACT THAT I'D BEEN CHOSEN...
IF I'D PAID ATTENTION TO THE PEOPLE COMING TO ME AS THE WATER PRIESTESS FOR HELP...
...I...
...MIGHT HAVE BEEN ABLE TO HELP YOU BACK THEN!
THAT'S WHY...
...I CAN'T LET GO!
I DON'T WANT TO REGRET LETTING YOU GO AS WELL!!

NGH...
HNNNGH!
TUG TUG
CRAP...
VSH VSH

SHLUP
KOFF
TCH
WE CAN'T LET YOU DO AS YOU PLEASE ANY LONGER.
SHUU

YOU...!
THE GODS!
YOU DID VERY WELL.

NOW GO OUT-SIDE.
ASAHI!
VSH
I WON'T LET YOU GO...!
FOOM
PEOPLE DON'T LIKE GUYS WHO DON'T LET UP...
...GOD OF DARK-NESS!

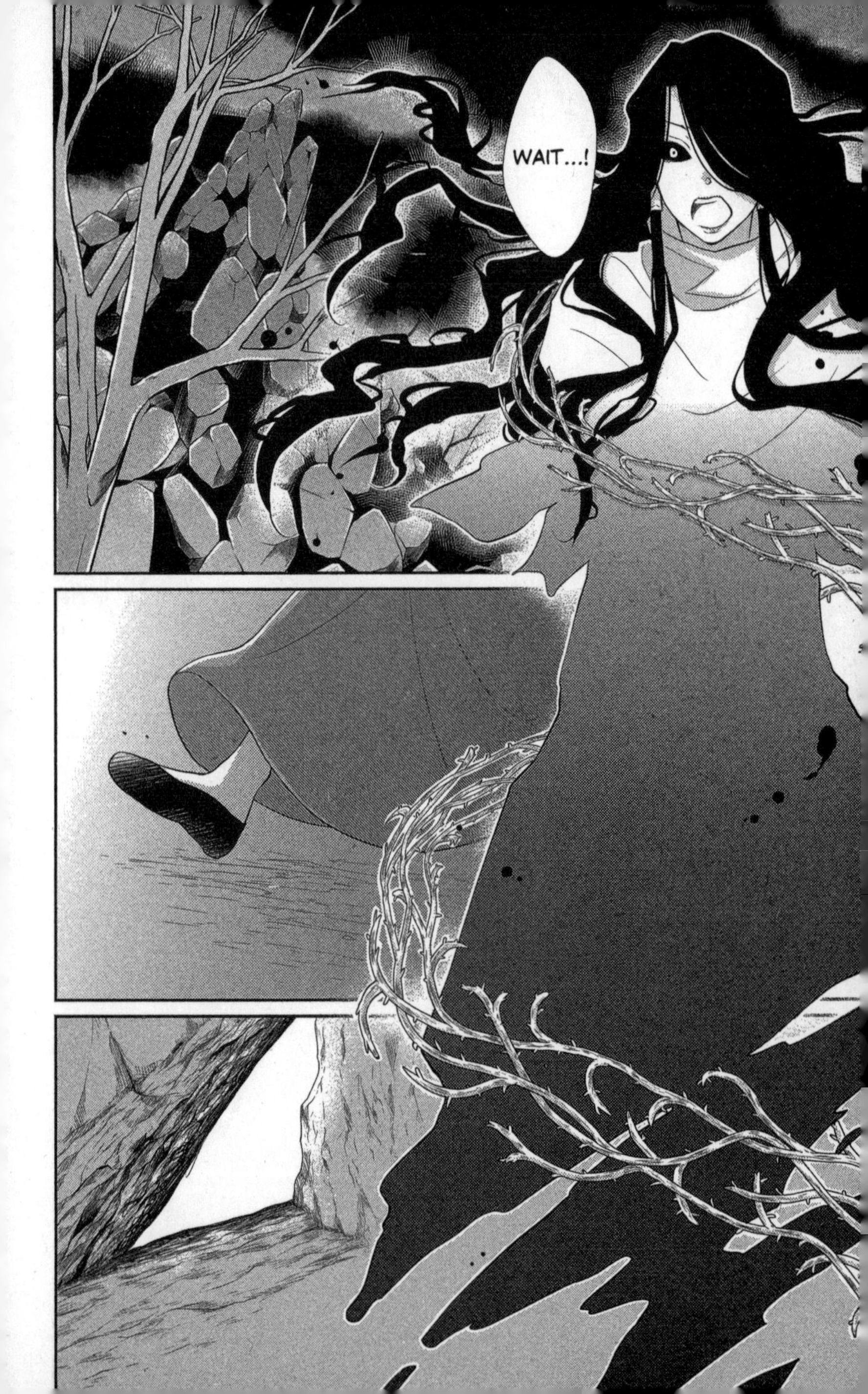
WAIT...!

THIS IS...
AHH...!
BWSH
WE WILL LEND YOU THE POWER TO SEAL AWAY THE GOD OF DARKNESS.

PLEASE SEAL HIM AWAY IN THE NAME OF THE WATER PRIESTESS.
UH...
HUH?
YOU SEE...
THIS HAS INVOLVED HUMANS TOO MUCH.
THAT IS TO SAY, WE NEED HUMAN POWER TO SETTLE THIS NOW.
SO LET US SEAL AWAY...
...THE GOD OF DARK-NESS.

SHF
N...
N...
NOOOO!

NGH...
DARKNESS WILL REMAIN.
FROM THE MOMENT THE SUN SHINES FORTH, DARKNESS IS ALREADY THERE.

HA
HA HA
HA HA
HA

SHAA

HEY
You've got a lot of nerve wasting our time!
Let's grow flowers here as well.
Oh... How lovely.
HEY
THESE... ARE GODS...?
They're so easy-going...
CHATTER CHATTER
How about some pink flowers here?
SHF
ASAHI, HOW IN THE WORLD DID YOU—

WE HOLD SOME RESPONSIBILITY FOR THE DECEPTIONS THAT THE GOD OF DARKNESS VISITED UPON THE HUMAN WORLD.
PERISH THE THOUGHT ...!
THIS WORLD, WITH ITS PROPENSITY TO GROW DARKNESS IN THE HEARTS OF HUMANS, IS THE TRUE SOURCE.
IN OTHER WORDS, AS THE EMPEROR OF THIS WORLD, I HAVE SHOWN MY UNWORTHINESS...!
HMM ...
WHEN ONE IS TOUCHED BY ANOTHER'S DEATH ...
...ONE IS TOUCHED BY THE DARKNESS OF THE HUMAN WORLD.
TOUCHED BY IT AS PART OF THE HUMAN WORLD.
EVEN AS YOU FIND JOY...
...PLEASE DO NOT FORGET THE PITIFUL GOD OF DARKNESS.
BECAUSE DARKNESS IS EVER BY YOUR SIDE.

HOW DO YOU PLAN TO MANAGE THAT DARKNESS ?
WE SHALL SEE.
YES!

HEY...
... TOKOYAMI.
AT THE BEGINNING...
... YOU SAVED MY LIFE, RIGHT?

YOU FOUND ME...
ARE YOU ENJOYING YOURSELF?
YEAH!
THIS IS FUN!
WHAT WAS THAT?
WERE YOU...
...HAVING FUN TOO?

YOU DON'T HAVE A NAME?
I HAVE NO NEED OF ONE.
THEN I'LL THINK OF ONE FOR YOU.
Hmm...
HOW ABOUT TOKO-YAMI?! IT MEANS "EVER-LASTING DARK-NESS."

IT'S... RATHER SIMPLE.
HA HA!
LET'S GO...
... TOKO-YAMI.
AHH...

THEY'RE STILL THERE...
...SHINING...
...WHITE.

I'M SORRY...
...TOKOYAMI.

CHAPTER
39

OUR TRUE RULER HAS RETURNED TO SAVE US FROM THE DARKNESS!
EMPEROR...!
YOUR MAJESTY...!
HURRAH
HURRAH
WATER PRIEST-ESS!

SILENCE
COME ON, ASAHI.
UM...
AH...
DO YOU STILL LACK AWARE-NESS OF YOUR STATUS ...
...MY PRIEST-ESS?

LADY PRIEST-ESS ...!!
THANK YOU!!
LADY PRIEST-ESS...!!
HURRAH
HURRAH
HOORAY

P-PLEASE FORGIVE US...!
YOUR MAJESTY ...!
HOW ARE WE GOING TO DEAL WITH THESE MEN?
HMM...
RUMORS WERE WHISPERED IN YOUR EARS BY EVIL ONES?
Y-YES, THAT'S RIGHT. IT WAS AS IF OUR MINDS WERE BEFOGGED.

VERY WELL.
I BELIEVE YOU.
I UNDERSTAND THAT EVEN AS YOU WERE BEING MISLED BY THE DESIRES IN YOUR HEART, THE LAUDABLE DESIRE TO MAKE THE COUNTRY STRONGER ALSO FUELED YOUR ACTIONS.
SINCE I WISH TO USE THAT DESIRE FOR OUR COUNTRY IN THE FUTURE...
...I WILL OVERLOOK YOUR CRIMES.

YOUR MAJESTY ...!
AND NOW... TO THE MASTER-MIND WHO CREATED ALL THIS CONFUSION ...
... KUROSE.
BECAUSE YOU WERE CON-TROLLED BY AN EVIL POWER AS WELL...
...ANY PUNISH-MENT VISITED UPON YOU WOULD HAVE TO BE VISITED UPON ALL THE OTHERS UNDER THAT SAME EVIL CONTROL.
EVEN SO, I CANNOT IGNORE YOUR CRIME IN BRINGING THIS DISTUR-BANCE TO MY COUNTRY.
THERE-FORE...

...I HEREBY BANISH YOU FROM THE CAPITAL.
YOU WILL NEVER BE ALLOWED TO ENTER THIS CITY AGAIN.
THAT'S... ALL?

ARE YOU REALLY GOING HOME?
YES... YOU DON'T NEED ANY MORE MIRACLES FROM GODS OR A PRIESTESS TO LEGITIMIZE YOU, DO YOU?
OF COURSE NOT!
THANK YOU...FOR HOW YOU DEALT WITH KUROSE.
HMPH. AS I SAID, ANY PUNISHMENT FOR HIS CRIMES WOULD ALSO HAVE TO BE VISITED UPON MY OWN BROTHER OUT OF FAIRNESS.
YOUR MAJESTY ...

I'M HAPPY TO JOIN MY HANDS...
...WITH THE EMPEROR YOU ARE NOW.

LADY PRIESTESS ...!

WELCOME BACK HOME, LADY ASAHI.
TSUKI-HIKO!

DOES COMING HERE... MAKE YOU UNHAPPY?
...
NOT REALLY.
NONE OF YOU REALLY DID ANYTHING WRONG. I KNOW THAT.
I SEE.
COME WITH ME. I'VE READIED A ROOM FOR YOU AT MY HOME.

OH, SUBARU!
MOTHER.
I HEARD FROM THE EMPEROR THAT YOU DID GREAT WORK AT HIS SIDE.
NOW OUR FAMILY'S FORTUNE IS SECURED.
OH HO HO HO HO HO
THAT... WAS YOUR MOTHER?
HM...? AH... WELL, YES.

SHE'S... CAUSED ME A LOT OF HEADACHES, TO SAY THE LEAST.
HA HA...
HEH
LOOKS LIKE BOTH OF US HAVE SUFFERED BECAUSE OF OUR MOTHERS.
HA HA... YOU TOO, HUH?

WATER ...
... DRAGON ...
...GOD!

SPLOOOSH

WATER DRAGON GOD!
WHAT'S THE MATTER?

I WANT TO SLEEP HERE WITH YOU.
IS THAT RIGHT?
YEP!

GOOD MORNING, WATER DRAGON GOD.
GOOD MORN-ING.

DON'T YOU HAVE TO GO HOME?
I MADE SURE TO TELL TSUKIHIKO I'D BE GONE.
AH... NO.

I SEE.
OH, I KNOW!
LET'S PLAY HIDE-AND-SEEK!
WHAT IS THAT?
I'LL HIDE SOMEWHERE...
...AND THEN YOU COME FIND ME.
OKAY? JUST WAIT A LITTLE AND THEN COME LOOK FOR ME.
OKAY, COME FIND ME!

...
IS THIS... FUN?
NOT AT ALL!
Cheater!!
PFF

WILL YOU BE SLEEPING HERE AGAIN?
YEAH.
DO YOU WANT ME TO GO HOME?

IF YOU INSIST ON CONTINUING TO BREAK THE MONOTONY WITH FOOLISH GAMES, PERHAPS.
HEY! I ALREADY SAID I WAS SORRY FOR MAKING YOU GO ALONG WITH IT!
HE'S THE SAME AS EVER.
HE SEEMS TO BE WATCHING ME...
...WITH THOSE COOL EYES.
THEIR COLOR IS LIKE THE BOTTOM OF THE OCEAN...
A DEEP BLUE.

THOSE EYES ARE SOMETIMES SO CRUEL...
...BUT SOMETIMES SO KIND.
WHAT THE GOD OF DARK-NESS SAID...
"YOU COULD NEVER UNDER-STAND..."
"...THIS..."

I KNOW WHAT HE WANTED TO SAY.
THAT I COULD NOT UNDERSTAND...
...HIS LONELI-NESS.
THE LONELINESS OF SPENDING AN ETERNITY...
...IN SOLI-TUDE.
IF I HAD NEVER MET YOU...
...I WOULD HAVE NEVER UNDER-STOOD THAT FEELING.

BUT...
YOU STILL...
...DON'T UNDERSTAND.
YOU DON'T UNDERSTAND HOW SAYING THINGS LIKE THAT...
...MAKES IT IMPOSSIBLE FOR ME TO FIGURE OUT MY FEELINGS.
WHICH HOME...
...SHOULD I GO BACK TO?

GOOD NIGHT.
CAN I STAY HERE LIKE THIS...
...FOREVER?
NNH...

IT'S SO BEAUTIFUL...
I FEEL LIKE...
...I COULD MELT INTO THIS WATER...
THE SAME WAY I FADE INTO A DREAM...

GOOD MORNING, WATER DRAGON GO—

NO WAY...
THE WATER DRAGON GOD...
...IS SLEEP-ING...?

WATER DRAGON GOD...
WATER DRAGON GOD?
HEY.
FWP
HEY!
WATER DRAGON GOD!

IMPOSSIBLE.

I'VE NEVER SEEN HIM SLEEP BEFORE, NOT EVEN ONCE.
BECAUSE HE DOESN'T NEED TO SLEEP.

COULD IT BE THAT HIS POWER IS...?
FWSH
OH NO...
OH
WATER DRAGON GOD...

BLOOSH
HE MELTED INTO THE WATER...
FADING...
JUST LIKE A DREAM...

My back hurts.
The stoop-shouldered posture I have when I draw keeps getting worse and worse. Recently when I finished drawing, I went to bed like usual, but when I woke up my back was hurting and I had an upset stomach. It was the first time I'd ever felt pain like that, so I was worried something had happened... I went to a massage clinic and immediately felt so much better. The whole thing shocked me, and I was like, "I have to be more careful..."
But of course, I'm back to drawing with my shoulders stooped over. What a fool I am...
Emperor

CHAPTER
40

WATER DRAGON GOD...
WATER DRAGON GOD...?
WHERE DID YOU GO?
HEY...!

SPLASH

SUBARU ...!
HUFF HUFF
ASAHI? WHAT...
HAVE YOU SEEN THE WATER DRAGON GOD?!
NO... I HAVEN'T...
WHAT'S WRONG? WEREN'T YOU WITH HIM...?

THE WATER DRAGON GOD DISAPPEARED ...!
I CAN'T FIND HIM ANYWHERE!
HE WAS ASLEEP ...
SOME-THING'S DEFINITELY WRONG!
I CAN'T BELIEVE HE JUST SUDDENLY DISAP-PEARED LIKE THAT!
ASA...
ASAHI!

SNAP
OW...!
THWUMP
ASAHI!
ARE YOU OKAY?
ASAHI ...
SHA
OH... YOU POOR THING...

TREE GOD...
TREE GOD... THE WATER DRAGON GOD, HE...!
IT'S ALL RIGHT. HE'S WITH US.

PLEASE, COME ALONG.

THERE YOU ARE.
WATER DRAGON GOD...!

WATER DRAGON GOD...
WHY...
WHY IS HE SLEEPING ...?!
HE'S NEVER DONE THIS BEFORE!
THERE WAS A TIME WHEN THE WATER DRAGON GOD TOOK YOU INTO HIMSELF, CORRECT?
THAT WAS... WELL, IN SOME SENSE...

...HIM DEVOURING YOU.
AND HE BECAME ONE WITH YOU.
THE TWO OF YOU BLENDED TOGETHER.
HIS GODLY POWER BEGAN TO FLOW INTO YOU...
...AND HE BECAME WEAKENED.

WHAT ...?
DO YOU REMEMBER THE TIMES YOU USED HIS POWER?
"THIS IS PROBABLY THE WATER DRAGON GOD'S POWER."
"OTHER GODS CAN'T ENTER THIS PLACE."
WAS THAT ME... CALLING THE WATER DRAGON GOD...?

KUROSE BECAME WEAKER WHEN THE DARK MIASMA TOUCHED HIM.
I WONDER IF YOU WERE ALL RIGHT BECAUSE YOU HAD THE POWER OF THE WATER GOD INSIDE YOU...
OTHER-WISE YOU WOULD HAVE GOTTEN WEAK TOO.
W-WHAT DO I DO?!
IF THIS KEEPS UP, WHAT'S GOING TO HAPPEN TO THE WATER DRAGON GOD?!
A RENEWED GOD OF WATER WILL LIKELY BE BORN.

AFTER HE FADES AWAY, THAT IS.
BUT... NO...
FADES... AWAY...?
HOWEVER ...

IF THE TWO OF YOU BECOME ONE COMPLETELY...
...HE MIGHT NOT DISAPPEAR.
BECOME ONE...?
YOU WOULD BE HIS SACRIFICE.

BUT... IT'S NOT A GUARANTEE.
WE DON'T KNOW FOR SURE.
IT'S OUR FIRST TIME ENCOUNTERING THIS.
THAT'S FINE!
ASAHI!

I'M ALL RIGHT WITH IT!
IT DOESN'T MATTER WHAT I HAVE TO DO.
BECAUSE I—
WHO...
...IS SAYING...
...SUCH FOOLISH THINGS?

WATER DRAGON GOD...!
THANK GOOD-NESS...

UM... HUH?
ARE YOU... MAD AT ME?

I WILL NOT ALLOW IT.
DO YOU UNDERSTAND?
BUT—!
SOMETHING I DID IS THE ORIGIN OF THIS ISSUE.
BUT BUT BUT...!!
YOU ARE A BAD LISTENER. I SAID YOU ARE NOT RESPONSIBLE FOR THIS MATTER.
I KNOW, BUT...

I HAVE NO INTENTION OF EATING YOU.
WATER DRAGON GOD!
TOSS
YOU GUYS CAN WORK THIS OUT ON YOUR OWN FROM HERE.
DO WHATEVER YOU WANT TO DO.

FWP
...
...
FOR NOW, LET'S GO BACK HOME.
WE DON'T KNOW WHEN THE WATER DRAGON GOD WILL FALL ASLEEP AGAIN.
Y-YEAH...
NHN...
WHAT'S WRONG?
THOSE WOUNDS ...

CLIMB ON MY BACK, ASAHI.
I'LL—
FWSH

BUCKLE
FWUP
YOU ARE HEAVY.
W—
I-I-I-I AM NOT!
I'M NORMAL!
NO, YOU ARE HEAVY.
IT'S ONLY BECAUSE YOU'RE LOSING YOUR POWER!!

...
...
FLEX
GRP
ZZZ
HEY.

IF YOU REALLY DID DEVOUR ASAHI...
...I WOULDN'T LET YOU GET AWAY WITH IT.

WERE I TO DO SOMETHING TO HARM THAT ONE...
...I WOULD LIKE YOU...
...TO PLEASE KILL ME.

THEN I WILL.

AHH...
PLEASE...

EVEN THOUGH THE GODS THEMSELVES...
...HAVE NO CONTROL OVER THIS...
...STILL...
...I'LL PRAY...
...THAT SOMEHOW...
...THESE TWO...
...WHO ARE SO DEVOTED TO ONE ANOTHER...
...WILL END UP HAPPY.

HNH...
FWUP

...MN.
GOOD MORN-ING.
WHAT A STRANGE FEELING.
SO THIS IS WAKING UP...
PFFH
BED HEAD !!
WHAT IS IT?

HEH
HA HA
AH HA
HA HA HA
...
HA HA HA HA
AHH... THAT WAS SO FUNNY.
...

WATER DRAGON GOD.
...
LET'S HAVE BREAK-FAST.
I'LL BRING SOME FOR YOU.

YOU'VE STARTED TO SLEEP JUST LIKE PEOPLE DO...
...AND YOU'RE GETTING ALL WIMPY AND WEAK...
Wimpy...?
DOES THAT MEAN YOU'RE BECOMING HUMAN?
I AM NOT HUMAN. BUT IT SEEMS THAT AS MY POWER FLOWS INTO YOU...
...YOUR HUMANLIKE SENSATIONS ARE FLOWING INTO ME AS WELL.
HOW STRANGE...
HUH?
IT'S DIFFER-ENT...
...FROM WHAT I ATE LAST TIME...
HUH...

IT DOESN'T TASTE UNPLEASANT.
MNCH
MEDICINAL JELLY
THAT FOOD...
...FROM LAST TIME
TH-TH-THAT WAS...
...A FAILED EXPERIMENT, I TOLD YOU!
Hmm... So that's what you call a bad taste, then...
CLATTER

WHAT'S THE MATTER?
SO YOU'VE BEEN ABLE...
...TO TASTE SINCE THEN...?
?
THMP

WHAT ...?
DO YOU...
...FEEL PAIN TOO...?

WHAT IS IT?
WHY ARE YOU CRYING?
NGH...
HNF...
I'M...
...SOR...

SORRY
...
WATER DRAGON GOD...
DON'T CRY.
...
WATER DRAGON GOD...?!

MY CHEST...
IT... HURTS.
THE WATER DRAGON'S BRIDE 10 – THE END –

The truth is...

The next volume will be the last volume of *The Water Dragon's Bride*!

I hope you keep reading until the end.

Rei Toma

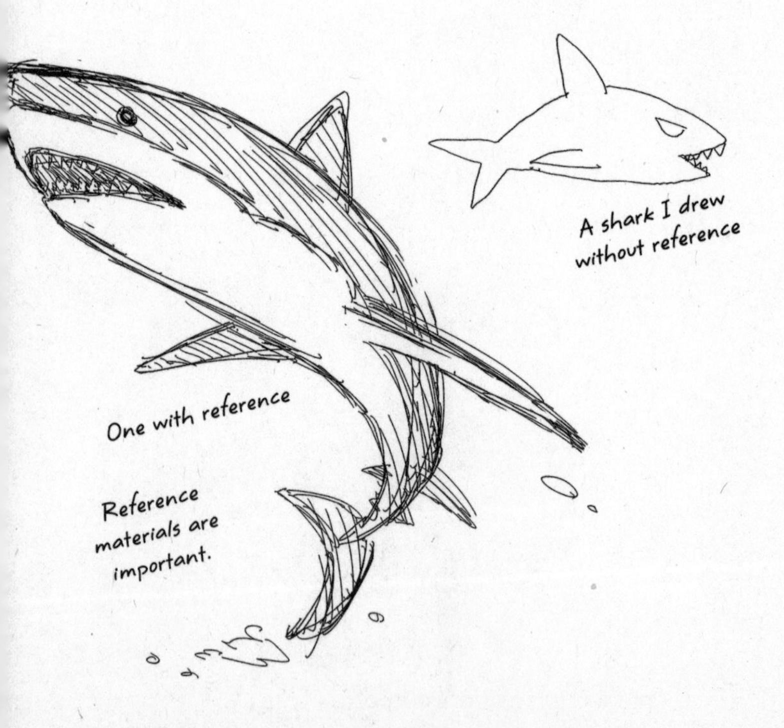

A shark I drew without reference
One with reference
Reference materials are important.

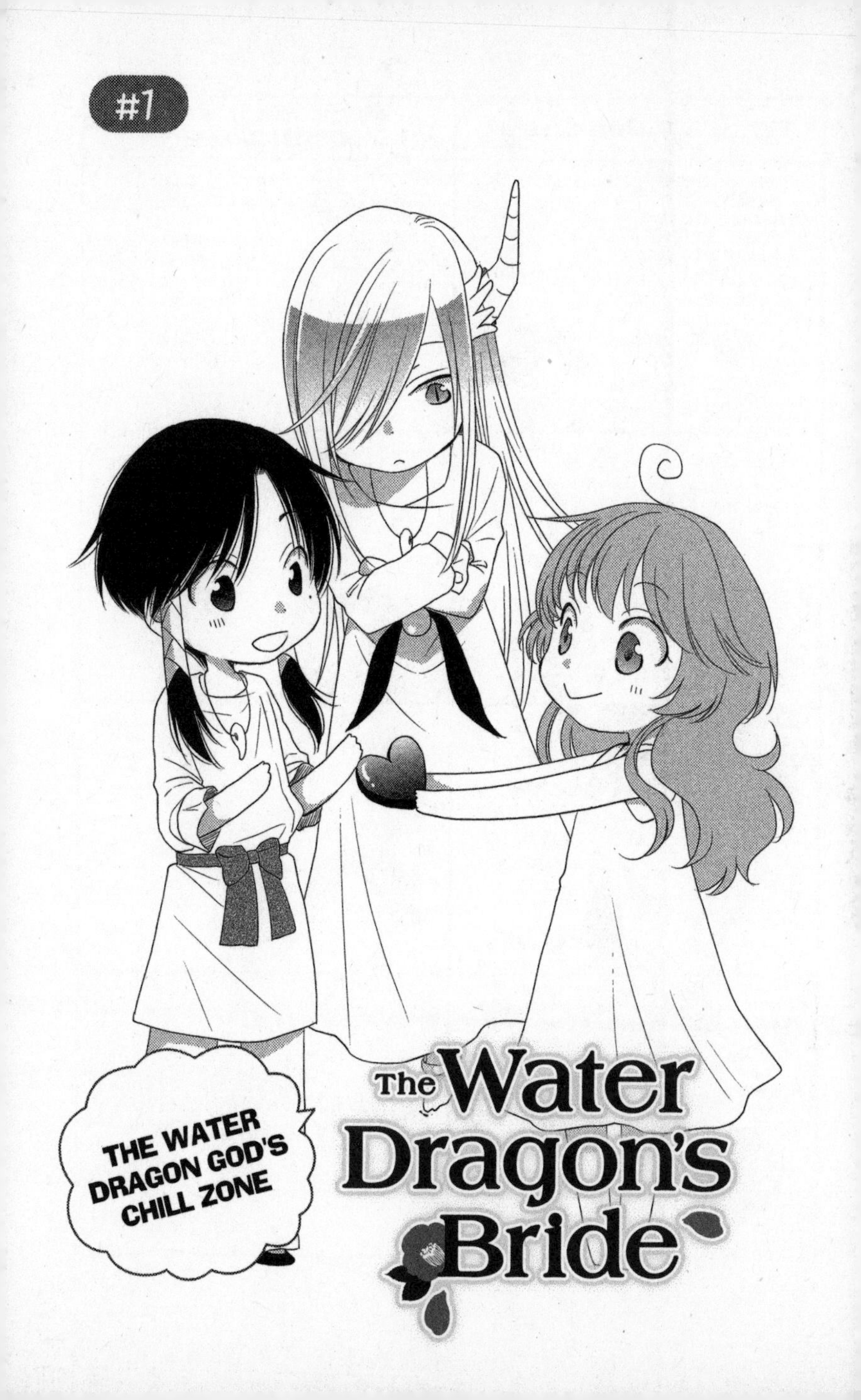
#1
THE WATER DRAGON GOD'S CHILL ZONE
The Water Dragon's Bride

Because It's the Chill Zone
AHH... I WANT TO EAT SOMETHING SWEET.
WHAT DO YOU WANT TO EAT? PERSIMMONS?
NO! I WANT CAKE OR CHOCOLATE OR SOMETHING LIKE THAT!
CHOK-LIT?
WHICH MEANS THAT THIS TIME WE'RE GOING TO DO A HEART-POUNDING VALENTINE'S CHOCOLATE EDITION! ♡
ANYTHING IS POSSIBLE HERE.
*THIS COMIC HAS NOTHING TO DO WITH THE ACTUAL STORY.
What's Valentine's?
VAL-UN-TIME? CHOK-LIT?
YOU GIVE THE SWEET TREAT CHOCOLATE TO PEOPLE YOU LIKE ON VALENTINE'S DAY.
HERE, FOR YOU, SUBARU!
HUH?!
B-BMP
TH-THIS IS FOR... SOMEONE YOU LIKE? WHICH MEANS...
A-ASAHI...
B-BMP
B-BMP
AH, BY THE WAY, VALENTINE'S DAY IS SUCH A BIG EVENT THAT THERE'S ALSO THIS THING CALLED OBLIGATORY CHOCOLATE. IT'S NONROMANTIC, AND EVERYONE JUST ENJOYS THE PRACTICE. SOME PEOPLE GIVE CHOCOLATE OUT TO BASICALLY EVERYONE.
DID YOU REALLY NEED TO TELL ME THAT NOW?

Finally, the Tasting!
ANYWAY, PLEASE TRY MY HANDMADE CHOCOLATE!
FONDLY
HMM... IT REALLY TAKES COURAGE...
So black...
CHOMP
TH-THIS... IS SO SWEET AND RICH...!
IT'S SO DELI-CIOUS, ASAHI!
YOU'RE A GENIUS TO BE ABLE TO MAKE THIS BY HAND...
WELL, I CALLED IT HANDMADE, BUT REALLY ALL I DID WAS MELT STORE-BOUGHT CHOCOLATE AND PUT IT INTO MOLDS. ACTUALLY, I'M MORE INTERESTED IN FINDING OUT HOW SOMEONE COULD MESS IT UP! I THINK IT'D BE TOUGH TO DO IT WRONG.
STOP SAYING STUFF THAT'S GOING TO MAKE ALL THE GIRLS IN THE COUNTRY HATE YOU, ASAHI!!
It's pretty dubious to call something like this handmade.
HONEST
What's Chocolate?
I DON'T REALLY KNOW WHAT CHOCOLATE IS TO BEGIN WITH, THOUGH.
NO WORRIES, JUST TRY THIS AND SEE!
Here.
I don't either.
I WONDER WHAT IT'S LIKE!
OOH
WARM
DOOM
I-IT'S BLACK...
THIS KINDA LOOKS LIKE POO—
HEY, CUT IT OUT.
I'll kill you.
It really does.

YOU CERTAINLY ENJOY COOKING...
YEAH.
I ALSO LIKE EATING.
WHEN SOMEONE EATS SOMETHING DELICIOUS, THEY JUST NATURALLY SMILE.
IT MAKES ME REALLY HAPPY TO SEE PEOPLE HAPPILY EATING THE FOOD I'VE MADE FOR THEM.
I DON'T UNDER-STAND.
HEE HEE
I DON'T REALLY EXPECT YOU COULD UNDER-STAND IT, WATER DRAGON GOD.

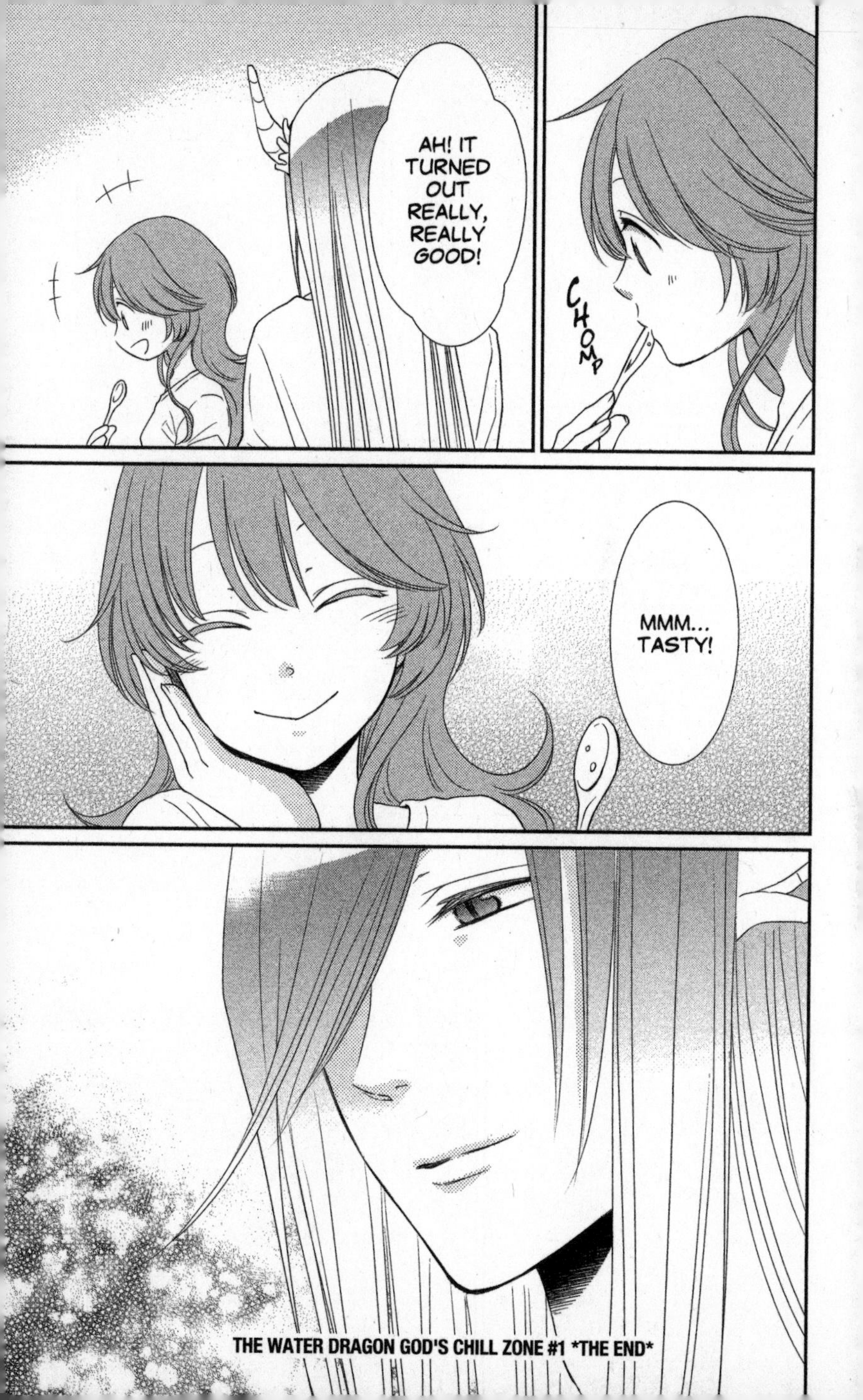
CHOMP
AH! IT TURNED OUT REALLY, REALLY GOOD!
MMM... TASTY!
THE WATER DRAGON GOD'S CHILL ZONE #1 *THE END*

#2
LOVE♥LO
The Water Dragon's Bride
THE WATER DRAGON GOD'S CHILL ZONE

*THIS COMIC HAS NOTHING TO DO WITH THE ACTUAL STORY.

MR. TSUKI-HIKO... THIS IS SO... I'M...
I'M JUST REPAYING YOU FOR VALENTINE'S DAY.
LET'S KEEP THIS A SECRET FROM THE OTHER STUDENTS, OKAY?
OF COURSE... MY HEART JUST WON'T STOP POUNDING...
S-SORRY... I WAS SO CONFUSED, AND I WASN'T SURE WHAT TO GET YOU.
SUBARU... I'M SO HAPPY.
WOW... MY HEART'S GOING PITTER-PATTER...
EAT AS MANY AS YOU LIKE.
HWAAAH!?

HWAAH!
HWAAH...
...
...
...
AHH... I HAD A REALLY WEIRD DREAM.
WHAT HAPPENED?
HM? UM... HMM... I CAN'T REMEMBER.
BUT NOW I'M TIRED...
...AND I CAN'T GET BACK TO SLEEP.
SHIFT SHIFT

NGH...
NHN NHN
SHIFT SHIFT
NHN NHN
SHIFT SHIFT
WHAT'S THIS, WATER DRAGON GOD?
FWSH
WHO KNOWS.
FWSH
NNN...
THE WATER DRAGON GOD'S CHILL ZONE #2 *THE END*

The next volume will be the last!
Thank you for all your support!

– REI TOMA

Rei Toma has been drawing since childhood, and she created her first complete manga for a graduation project in design school. When she drew the short story manga "Help Me, Dentist," it attracted a publisher's attention and she made her debut right away. After she found success as a manga artist, acclaim in other art fields started to follow as she did illustrations for novels and video game character designs. She is also the creator of *Dawn of the Arcana*, available in North America from VIZ Media.

The Water Dragon's Bride

VOL. 10

Shojo Beat Edition

Story and Art by

Rei Toma

SUIJIN NO HANAYOME Vol.10
by Rei TOMA

Original Japanese edition published by SHOGAKUKAN.
English translation rights in the United States of America, Canada, the United Kingdom, Ireland, Australia and New Zealand arranged with SHOGAKUKAN.

ORIGINAL COVER DESIGN/Hibiki CHIKADA (fireworks.vc)

English Translation & Adaptation **Abby Lehrke**
Touch-Up Art & Lettering **Monaliza de Asis**
Design **Alice Lewis**
Editor **Amy Yu**

Printed in the U.S.A.

Published by VIZ Media, LLC
P.O. Box 77010
San Francisco, CA 94107

10 9 8 7 6 5 4 3 2 1
First printing, July 2019

ratings.viz.com
RATED T TEEN

PARENTAL ADVISORY
THE WATER DRAGON'S BRIDE is rated T for Teen and is recommended for ages 13 and up. This volume contains suggestive themes.

viz.com

shojobeat.com

You may be reading the wrong way!

eeping with the original Japanese c format, this book reads from right eft—so action, sound effects and l balloons are completely reversed. is preserves the orientation of the original artwork—plus, it's fun!

ieck out the diagram shown here get the hang of things, and then urn to the other side of the book to get started!

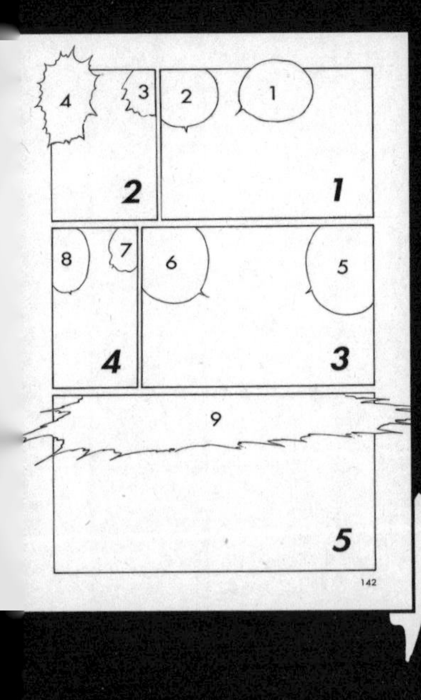